WOULD YOU RATHER?

CHRISTMAS EDITION

150+ FUN, FESTIVE, HILARIOUS
QUESTIONS FOR THE WHOLE FAMILY
TO ENJOY TOGETHER

MADE EASY PRESS

Producer & International Distributor
eBookPro Publishing
www.ebook-pro.com

Would You Rather? Christmas Edition:
150+ Fun, Festive, Hilarious Questions for the Whole Family to Enjoy Together

Made Easy Press

Copyright © 2023

All rights reserved; No parts of this book may be reproduced or transmitted in any form or by any means, electronic or mechanical, including photocopying, recording, taping, or by any information retrieval system, without the permission, in writing, of the author.

Cover and Illustrations: Maria Sokhatski

Contact: agency@ebook-pro.com
ISBN

HOW TO PLAY

"Would You Rather: Christmas Edition"

Would You Rather is a fun, simple game for the whole family to play together. This festive edition is perfect for family holiday game night, Christmas morning, or your annual holiday party. However you are celebrating, *Would You Rather* is a hilarious, creative, fun activity that will get you in the holiday mood!

Who Can Play?

Anyone can play this family-friendly edition of the popular game – kids, parents, grandparents, friends. All of the questions are kid-and-family-friendly!

How Many Players Do You Need?

You need at least two players to properly play the game, but there is no such thing as too many players! You can even read the book on your own if you want to, it just won't really feel like a game, more like a personal challenge.

The Questions

This book features 150 Would You Rather questions. Each question will present you with two cheery, joyful, Christmassy choices to consider.

The Rules

Each round, choose one person to be the judge. After the first round, we recommend you go around the circle in a clockwise direction.

The judge looks at the page and asks everyone the Would You Rather question out loud. For example:

Would you rather be best friends with Frosty the Snowman or be best friends with Rudolph the Reindeer?

Give everyone a minute to think about their answer, and then go around the table with everyone explaining what they would choose, and why.

This is where you can get creative – try to think of the smartest, funniest, and silliest explanations, because the person whose answer is deemed best by the judge will win the round!

After everyone has given their answer, the judge rules who gave the best answer and that person receives one point.

Use a piece of paper or a whiteboard to keep score every round!

The Winner

You can choose to play the whole book or just a part of it – either way, once you're done, tally up the points from all the rounds to see who the winner is!

2-Player Game

If you are playing with only two players, take turns being the judge each time. Give each other points between 1 and 3, according to how much you liked the answer. At the end of the game, the player with the most points wins.

Group Variation

Another way to play the game is in two groups. If there are a lot of players, say more than 8, you can divide up into two teams and play against one another. In this version of the game, one of the teams will ask the question and the other team will have to come up with an answer that they all agree on. The first team will then give them a score from 1 to 3, just like in the two-player game. Change turns after each question and count up the points as usual at the end of the game to see which team is the winner.

Would you rather...

Know what all your gifts
are in advance

or

Be surprised by all your gifts?

Would you rather...

Have tinsel for hair

or

Have Christmas lights
for fingernails?

Would you rather...

Live in a gingerbread house

or

Live in the North Pole with Santa?

Would you rather...

Eat cereal with eggnog

or

Eat a candy cane sandwich?

Would you rather...

Be as short as an elf

or

Be as big as a reindeer?

Would you rather...

Get ten small Christmas presents

or

Get one big Christmas present?

Would you rather...

Go to see the Nutcracker

or

Dance the main part
in the Nutcracker?

Would you rather...

Forget to buy someone
important a gift

or

Not receive a gift from
someone important?

Would you rather...

Receive five gold rings

or

Receive a partridge
in a pear tree?

Would you rather...

Be best friends
with Frosty the Snowman

or

Be best friends
with Rudolph the Reindeer?

Would you rather...

Sing Christmas carols
in the freezing snow

or

Perform in a Christmas
play underwater?

Would you rather...

Go Christmas shopping
for every single person you know

or

Not get any gifts for Christmas?

Would you rather...

Ride on a sled

or

Ride on a snowmobile?

Would you rather...

Celebrate Christmas at home
and get gifts

or

Celebrate Christmas at Disneyland
but not get any gifts?

Would you rather...

Eat s'mores with salty crackers instead of sweet crackers

or

Eat s'mores with ketchup instead of chocolate?

Would you rather...

Wrap fifty presents

or

Write fifty cards?

Would you rather...

Have eyes made out of coal

or

Have a carrot for a nose?

Would you rather...

Watch Christmas movies all day

or

Listen to Christmas songs all day?

Would you rather...

Visit Santa in the North Pole

or

Visit the Sugar Plum Fairy in the Nutcracker?

Would you rather...

Celebrate Christmas with your favorite character from a book

or

Celebrate Christmas with your favorite character from a movie?

Would you rather...

Dress up as Santa

or

Dress up as an elf?

Would you rather...

Take down the Christmas tree

or

Do all the dishes
after Christmas dinner?

Would you rather...

Invite the Grinch
for Christmas dinner

or

Get all your gifts
from the Grinch?

Would you rather...

Live inside a snow globe

or

Live inside a gingerbread house?

Would you rather...

Have gingerbread cookies for ears

or

Have candy canes for legs?

Would you rather...

Have the best Christmas tree
in the neighborhood

or

Have the best Christmas lights
in the neighborhood?

Would you rather...

Be a gingerbread man

or

Be a snowman?

Would you rather...

Gingerbread men came to life

or

The toys you got for Christmas came to life?

Would you rather...

Help Santa climb down a chimney

or

Help Santa fly his sleigh?

Would you rather...

Have a snowball fight
with a Transformer

or

Have a snowball fight
with the Hulk?

Would you rather...

Drink cold hot cocoa

or

Drink hot eggnog?

Would you rather...

Eat Christmas dinner with chopsticks

or

Eat Christmas dinner with your hands tied behind your back?

Would you rather...

Be the first person to fall asleep on Christmas Eve

or

Be the last person to fall asleep on Christmas Eve?

Would you rather...

Get stuck in a chimney

or

Get stuck in a stocking?

Would you rather...

Have a red nose like Rudolph

or

Have green fur like the Grinch?

Would you rather...

Stay home alone while
your family is on vacation

or

Have to defend your house
from intruders?

Would you rather...

Make a snow angel

or

Make a snowman?

Would you rather...

Help Santa wrap all the presents

or

Help Santa deliver all the presents?

Would you rather...

Wear a Christmas sweater
all year long

or

Wear 5 Christmas sweaters
on top of each other for one day?

Would you rather...

Have to eat a whole turkey
by yourself

or

Have to eat a whole Christmas
pudding by yourself?

Would you rather...

Have Christmas dinner at home with all your cousins

or

Have Christmas dinner at your cousins' house?

Would you rather...

Not have a Christmas tree

or

Not have Christmas cookies?

Would you rather...

Eat burnt Christmas pudding

or

Eat burnt Christmas turkey?

Would you rather...

Sleep outside in the snow

or

Eat all your meals outside in the snow?

Would you rather...

Have an advent calendar
with candy

or

Have an advent calendar
with books?

Would you rather...

Wash your face with cranberry sauce

or

Wash your hands with gravy?

Would you rather...

Eat turkey stuffed with candy canes

or

Eat turkey stuffed with gingerbread men?

Would you rather...

Make all the decorations for the Christmas tree yourself

or

Pay for all the decorations for the Christmas tree yourself?

Would you rather...

Find a worm in your Christmas dinner

or

Find a maggot in your hot cocoa?

Would you rather...

Write a popular Christmas song

or

Star in a popular Christmas movie?

Would you rather...

Get lost in a Christmas tree farm

or

Get lost in the mall while shopping for presents?

Would you rather...

Have all your Christmas tree lights the same color

or

Have all your Christmas tree lights different colors?

Would you rather...

Only speak in rhymes
the whole holiday

or

Only speak in song lyrics
the whole holiday?

Would you rather...

Wear an ugly Christmas
sweater to Church

or

Wear an elf's hat to Church?

Would you rather...

Take a bath in gravy

or

Take a shower in hot cocoa?

Would you rather...

Climb onto the roof to put up Christmas lights

or

Climb up a chimney to help Santa who's stuck?

Would you rather...

Only eat fruitcake
for dessert for a month

or

Not eat any dessert
for a month?

Would you rather...

All your presents were wrapped
in ten layers of wrapping paper

or

None of your presents
were wrapped at all?

Would you rather...

Compete in a professional gingerbread-eating competition

or

Compete in a professional snowball fight?

Would you rather...

Watch the Nutcracker ballet

or

Watch Disney on Ice?

Would you rather...

Watch the Nutcracker ballet

or

Watch Disney on Ice?

Would you rather...

Open one present
on Christmas eve

or

Open one present
the day after Christmas?

Would you rather...

Wear matching Christmas pajamas
with your whole family

or

Wear matching ugly sweaters
with your whole family?

Would you rather...

Go to school in an elf costume

or

Go to school in a Santa costume?

Would you rather...

Ride a reindeer to school

or

Ride the Polar Express to school?

Would you rather...

Go ice skating

or

Go skiing?

Would you rather...

Wear a Christmas wreath
around your neck like a necklace

or

Wear Christmas ornaments
from your ears like earrings?

Would you rather...

Listen to a Christmas choir

or

Sing in a Christmas choir?

Would you rather...

Listen to a Christmas choir

or

Sing in a Christmas choir?

Would you rather...

Get a Secret Santa gift from the Grinch

or

Get a Secret Santa gift from a gremlin?

Would you rather...

Decorate Christmas cookies with ketchup

or

Decorate Christmas cookies with toothpaste?

Would you rather...

Share all your presents with a sibling

or

Only get one present?

Would you rather...

Donate all your Christmas presents
to children in need

or

Donate all your Christmas food
to families in need?

Would you rather...

Build a giant snow fort
but have to live in it

or

Build a giant snowman
but have to take it with you
wherever you go?

Would you rather...

Have reindeer antlers
on your head

or

Have the Grinch's nose?

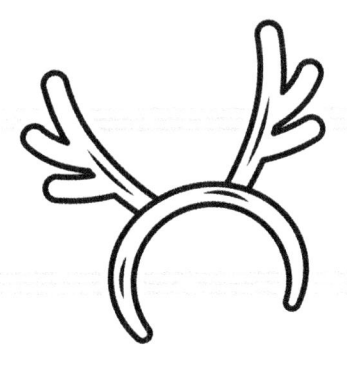

Would you rather...

Have elf ears

or

Have Santa's beard?

Would you rather...

Spend Christmas with Kevin McCallister from Home Alone

or

Spend Christmas with Anna, Elsa, and Olaf from Frozen?

Would you rather...

Give up one family holiday tradition

or

Make up one new family holiday tradition?

Would you rather...

Spend as much money
as you want in a toy store

or

Spend as much money
as you want in a book store?

Would you rather...

Travel back in time to a Christmas
in the past

or

Travel forward in time to a Christmas
in the future?

Would you rather...

Celebrate your birthday on Christmas

or

Celebrate Christmas on your birthday?

Would you rather...

Have mittens on your hands for a week

or

Have skis on your feet for a week?

Would you rather...

Your pet cat destroys
the Christmas tree

or

Your pet dog destroys
all your Christmas gifts?

Would you rather...

Decorate your whole room
with tinsel

or

Decorate your whole room
with mistletoe?

Would you rather...

Untangle twenty strings
of Christmas lights

or

Find the one light that doesn't work
in twenty strings?

Would you rather...

Only get money and no presents

or

Only get presents and no money?

Would you rather...

Get a cockroach
in your Christmas cracker

or

Get a glitter bomb
in your Christmas cracker?

Would you rather...

Melt like a snowman

or

Be eaten like a gingerbread man?

Would you rather...

Wrap a hundred presents

or

Decorate a hundred trees?

Would you rather...

Receive socks
as a Christmas present

or

Receive a toothbrush
as a Christmas present?

Would you rather...

Be snowed into
the house on Christmas

or

Have no snow
at all on Christmas?

Would you rather...

Eat ham for Christmas breakfast

or

Eat turkey for Christmas breakfast?

Would you rather...

Forget your lines in the school nativity play

or

Forget the words to the Christmas carols in the Church choir?

Would you rather...

Talk to an elf on the shelf

or

Talk to the angel on the Christmas tree?

Would you rather...

Spend Christmas at Hogwarts

or

Spend Christmas in Narnia?

Would you rather...

Kiss the Grinch
under the mistletoe

or

Kiss Rudolph the Reindeer
under the mistletoe?

Would you rather...

Pick out a Christmas gift for your teacher

or

Pick out a Christmas gift for your least favorite kid in school?

Would you rather...

Get a puppy for Christmas

or

Get a PlayStation for Christmas?

Would you rather...

Sneeze in the family holiday picture

or

Blink in the family holiday picture?

Would you rather...

Fall into a snowdrift

or

Fall into a pile of leaves?

Would you rather...

Listen to Jingle Bells
every day for a month

or

Listen to Oh Holy Night
every day for a month?

Would you rather...

Hang out with the Grinch

or

Hang out with the Ghost
of Christmas past?

Would you rather...

Eat gravy-flavored ice cream

or

Eat chocolate-flavored gravy?

Would you rather...

Ride on a reindeer

or

Ride on a polar bear?

Would you rather...

Unwrap a gift locked with zip ties

or

Unwrap a gift glued with superglue?

Would you rather...

Celebrate Christmas for one day

or

Celebrate Hanukkah for 8 days?

Would you rather...

Always know the perfect gift to get for others

or

Always get the perfect gift for you?

Would you rather...

Get snow inside your shoes

or

Get snow inside your ears?

Would you rather...

Donate all the gifts
you got for Christmas

or

Donate all the money
you got for Christmas?

Would you rather...

Work in Santa's workshop

or

Help him deliver gifts?

Would you rather...

Have dinner with Santa Claus

or

Have dinner with Mrs. Claus?

Would you rather...

Have to do your Christmas shopping early in January

or

Have to do your Christmas shopping the day before Christmas?

Would you rather...

Take down your Christmas decorations the day after Christmas

or

Keep your Christmas decorations up all year long?

Would you rather...

Receive only boring, practical gifts

or

Receive only fun, impractical gifts?

Would you rather...

Choose ten people to go
on Santa's nice list

or

Choose one person to go
on Santa's naughty list?

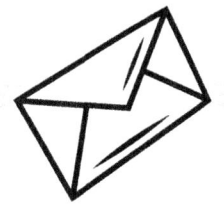

Would you rather...

Eat Christmas cookies with sprinkles
but no icing

or

Eat Christmas cookies with icing
but no sprinkles?

Would you rather...

All the holidays of the year
were in the same month

or

All the holidays were spread out
over the year?

Would you rather...

Spend Christmas Eve
at the White House

or

Spend Christmas Eve
in Buckingham Palace?

Would you rather...

Discover that your dad
is secretly Santa in disguise

or

Discover that your teacher
is secretly the Grinch in disguise?

Would you rather...

Wear a onesie the entire month
of December

or

Wear elf boots the entire month
of December?

Would you rather...

Have a small, real Christmas tree

or

Have a huge, plastic Christmas tree?

Would you rather...

Play mini golf with a candy cane

or

Play bowling with a marshmallow?

Would you rather...

Have a vegan Christmas dinner
with non-vegan dessert

or

Have a non-vegan Christmas dinner
with vegan dessert?

Would you rather...

Spend Christmas as an old person

or

Spend Christmas as a baby?

Would you rather...

Celebrate Christmas
for one day every year

or

Celebrate Christmas for two days
every other year?

Would you rather...

Have to dance every time
you hear a Christmas song

or

Have to sing every time
you hear a Christmas song?

Would you rather...

Cook a Christmas meal
for a hundred people

or

Clear up after a Christmas meal
for a hundred people?

Would you rather...

Spend Christmas day with someone
who hates Christmas

or

Spend Christmas day with someone
who won't stop talking?

Would you rather...

Fall into a holly bush

or

Trip over a string
of Christmas lights?

Would you rather...

Give one person a $100 gift

or

Give a hundred people a $1 gift?

Would you rather...

Find reindeer poop
in your shoes

or

Find coal in your stocking?

Would you rather...

Knit ten Christmas sweaters

or

Wear ten Christmas sweaters
all at once?

Would you rather...

Eat eggnog-flavored fruitcake

or

Drink fruitcake-flavored eggnog?

Would you rather...

Stay up all night trying to see Santa

or

Go to sleep quickly so you can wake up sooner?

Would you rather...

Wash you hair with hot chocolate

or

Take a bath in eggnog?

Would you rather...

Have a Christmas stocking that refills with treats every time you reach inside

or

Have a magic hat that gives you a new hairstyle every day?

Would you rather...

Smell like turkey

or

Smell like chimney soot?

Would you rather...

Wear Christmas stockings as socks

or

Wear a Christmas wreath as a belt?

Would you rather...

Get wrapped gifts from Santa Claus that are covered in pee

or

Get moldy potatoes from the Easter bunny instead of chocolate?

Would you rather...

Forget that it is Christmas until the day before

or

Forget that it is Christmas until the day after?

Would you rather...

Have a candy cane that never ends

or

Have a snow globe with snow that falls forever?

Would you rather...

Attend a Christmas party with your favorite cartoon characters

or

Attend a Christmas party with your favorite superheroes?

Would you rather...

Wake up and find out that Santa only brought you half your gifts

or

Wake up and find out that Santa didn't eat the cookies you left him?

Would you rather...

Spend Christmas in Australia

or

Spend Christmas in Hawaii?

Would you rather...

Have a snowball launcher
that shoots marshmallows

or

Have a Christmas cracker
that releases confetti?

Would you rather...

Meet a reindeer who can talk

or

Meet a snowman who can ice skate?

Would you rather...

Have a glow-in-the-dark
Christmas tree

or

Have a Christmas tree
that sparkles all day?

Would you rather...

Get a magical sleigh that takes you
anywhere you want

or

Get a pair of boots that let you
walk on clouds?

Would you rather...

Have a magical snow globe
that shows you any place in the world

or

Have a magical ornament
that grants wishes?

Would you rather...

Have Christmas in the summer

or

Have summer vacation in the winter?

Would you rather...

Only be able to celebrate
your birthday but not Christmas

or

Only be able to celebrate Christmas
but not your birthday?

Would you rather...

Find a rat in your
Christmas tree

or

Find a snake in your
Christmas stocking?

Would you rather...

Compete in a snowball fight
with your friends

or

Build a snow fort
with your family?

Would you rather...

Wake up to gummy bears
falling like snow from the sky

or

Wake up to marshmallows
falling like snow from the sky?

Printed in Great Britain
by Amazon